on duty

LIFE AS A PARATROOPER

Robert C. Kennedy

HIGH
interest
books

Children's Press
A Division of Grolier Publishing
New York / London / Hong Kong / Sydney
Danbury, Connecticut

Book Design: Nelson Sa
Contributing Editor: Mark Beyer
Photo Credits: Cover © The Miltary Picture Library/Corbis; p. 5 © Corbis; p. 7 © Leif Skoogfors/Corbis; p. 9 © Corbis; p. 10 © Corbis; p. 14 © Leif Skoogfors/Corbis; pp. 17, 18, 23, 25 © Corbis; p. 26 © Bettmann/Corbis; p. 29 © Corbis; pp. 31, 32 © Corbis; p. 34 © Peter Russell;The Miltary Picture Library/Corbis; p. 37 © Leif Skoogfors/Corbis; p. 39, 41 © Corbis.

Visit Children's Press on the Internet at:
http://publishing.grolier.com

Library of Congress Cataloging-in-Publication Data

Kennedy, Robert C.
    Life as a paratrooper / by Robert C. Kennedy.
        p. cm. – (On duty)
    Includes bibliographical references and index.
    Summary: Explains what it takes to become a paratrooper, discusses the
        combat history of the 82nd Airborne Division, and describes the training
        necessary for these special soldiers.
    ISBN 0-516-23344-0 (lib. bdg.) – ISBN 0-516-23544-3 (pbk.)
    1. United States. Army—Parachute troops—Juvenile literature. [1. United
        States.
    Army—Parachute troops. 2. Parachute troops.] I. Title. II. Series.

UD483.K45 2000
356'.166'0973—dc21
                                                        00-023801

CONTENTS

Introduction

The word parachute comes from the words parasol (an umbrella) and chute (to fall). The word paratrooper comes from the words parachute and trooper (a soldier). So, a paratrooper is an infantry soldier who parachutes into battle from an aircraft.

Soldiers in the U.S. Army's 82nd and 101st Airborne Divisions made the most famous parachute jumps in history. These jumps happened during World War II (1939-1945). The soldiers jumped the night before the United States and the Allies (group of friendly nations) invaded Germany to fight German forces. The paratroopers jumped into Belgium on the night of June 5th and the morning of June 6th, 1944. American infantry soldiers came ashore at Omaha Beach in Normandy, France. By noon on June 6th, U.S. infantry troops were attacking the Germans from the front. At the same time, the paratroopers were attacking from the rear.

Paratroopers saw action in World War II (1939–1945).

The German soldiers either surrendered or ran from the battlefield.

The 101st Airborne Division is now the U.S. military's only air assault division. Its soldiers drop into battle by ropes (rappel) or from helicopters. The 82nd Airborne Division is now the only paratrooper division in the U.S. Army.

Behind the Parachutist Badge

WHO THEY ARE

Paratroopers are men willing to serve their country. They are physically fit and looking for excitement. They like action. Sitting behind a desk or walking a guard post are not their idea of action. They want to see some of the world and have a few thrills. They want a job that makes them use their minds and bodies. When they go home on leave, they want to have exciting stories to tell their friends.

WHAT PARATROOPERS DO

The area where one army is fighting another army is called the forward edge of the battle area (FEBA). It also may be called the front line or the main line of resistance (MLR). Paratroopers jump beyond that line. They land behind the enemy. They are able to catch the

Paratroopers ready themselves for a mission by checking each other's gear.

enemy by surprise and strike fear into all of its soldiers. Once paratroopers are on the ground, they become infantry soldiers. When they attack from behind, the enemy doesn't know where to fight. The enemy doesn't know where the next strike may occur. Enemy soldiers on the front lines become fearful.

To scare the enemy even more, hundreds of dummy paratroopers are usually dropped in other areas. These dummies look like real paratroopers. Enemy ground troops think that many more soldiers are landing. Using dummy troops makes the enemy separate its own troops. They send troops to defend against forces that are not actually there. Dummies help to confuse the enemy.

Once on the ground, paratroopers quickly destroy radio towers and telephone lines. It may take weeks to rebuild these communications sources. Enemy soldiers cannot talk to each other. They are confused. They may still

Some paratroopers are landed by helicopter.

think all those dummy paratroopers are real troops.

When U.S. paratroopers jumped behind German lines in 1945, high winds blew them away from their landing points. They were scattered into small groups. They began to attack in small groups at different places. The Germans thought that American troops were everywhere!

Pataroopers learn how to jump in jump school.

HOW PARATROOPERS ARE CHOSEN

All paratroopers are volunteers. Soldiers volunteer for airborne infantry training when they first join the Army. Paratrooper volunteers are first trained in combat infantry boot camp. The training takes place at Fort Benning, Georgia.

By law, women cannot be combat soldiers. Therefore, women cannot become paratroopers. Paratrooper volunteers go straight into jump school when they finish basic training. The jump school adds three weeks to a soldier's training time at Fort Benning.

JUMP SCHOOL

Week One is Ground Week

Soldiers do their jump training from an aircraft door mock-up. This mock-up is on top of a 34-foot-high tower. Soldiers strap on parachute harnesses. All the harnesses are attached to a cable that leads from the mock-up door to the ground. The cable is called a lateral drift apparatus (LDA). The LDA makes soldiers drift (move) sideways after they jump from the tower. This teaches a parachutist how to handle the real kind of drift during parachuting. Each time the soldiers jump, they practice the parachute landing falls (PLFs). Paratroopers land by rolling forward as their feet hit the ground. They roll to lessen the hard impact from a parachute landing.

Paratrooper trainees must pass a physical fitness (strength and endurance) test at the end of weeks one and two. Therefore, the soldiers do physical training every day. They want to be at their strongest when they take the tests. The test at the end of week one is the same as the test for any boot camp soldier. A soldier must be able to run three miles and do one hundred sit-ups and fifty chin-ups.

Week Two is Tower Week

During tower week, soldiers jump from a 250-foot-high tower. They wear parachutes. They must learn what it feels like to fall through the air and pull the chute cord. They are learning how to free-fall. Each soldier must become used to the feeling of falling through the air.

During the first week, soldiers learned how to land and roll. During the second week, they learn two other kinds of landings. The first new landing is the slant landing. The wind often blows a paratrooper sideways as he is falling from the sky. Many times he will not be moving forward as he lands. If he does not know how to land properly while moving sideways, he could break his legs or a hip. During a slant landing, a paratrooper must reach up and grab the wide belts (risers) that are connected to the parachute. By pulling the risers, he lifts his body and turns to face in the direction that he is moving. He wants to learn how to face forward so that he can land and roll.

The second type of landing is the strong wind landing. Strong winds can make landing from a parachute very difficult. Sometimes a paratrooper is moving forward at ten or fifteen miles per hour when he lands. To land

Paratroopers jump in groups. They must work together as a team.

properly, a paratrooper must have his legs moving when he hits the ground! Once on the ground, the paratrooper must quickly pull the chute cords toward him. This collapses the chute. Then the high wind doesn't pull the parachute and the paratrooper along the ground.

Teamwork

A group of paratroopers may jump from a plane at the same time. This is called a mass exit jump. Mass exit jumps are used when paratroopers want to stay close together while parachuting to the ground. They don't want to get separated by landing in different areas. Paratroopers must learn teamwork to do the mass exit jump. They learn to trust one another and to work together.

Overcoming Fear

No paratrooper is fearless, but a paratrooper learns to face fear. He must learn to control his emotions. When fear tries to take control of a paratrooper's actions, he concentrates on his mission. Once focused on the mission, he does his job. Each time he faces fear and conquers it, he learns how to overcome his fears. A paratrooper doesn't ignore the danger in any situation. However, he never lets danger or fear keep him from doing what he knows has to be done to accomplish a mission.

Week Three is Jump Week

Paratroopers are required to make five parachute jumps from an aircraft. Paratroopers sit in the plane wearing their parachute gear. They wear army combat uniforms (fatigues). They wear parachute harnesses. The harnesses are attached to the parachutes. Parachutes sit firmly on their backs.

A green light at the front of the plane comes on. The paratroopers line up at the door. An overhead cable (static line) runs from the front

Paratroopers must make five jumps during jump week.

to the back of the plane. The paratroopers hook their chute cords (rip cords) onto the static line. When they jump from the plane, rip cords are pulled by the static line. Their chutes open and the paratroopers drift slowly to the ground.

During training, paratroopers do not jump when winds are more than twelve to fourteen miles per hour. The U.S. Army will not risk having men jump during these dangerous conditions. However, during a military operation, paratroopers must jump during any condition if they are needed.

Each paratrooper team has two riflemen.

The five jumps are taken between Monday and Thursday. On Friday morning of jump week, the paratroopers go through a brief graduation ceremony. Then they leave for Fort Bragg, North Carolina, where the U.S. Army's only airborne (paratrooper) corps is stationed.

HOW PARATROOPS
ARE ORGANIZED

At Fort Bragg, paratroopers are assigned to a rifle fire team. The team leader is a corporal or sergeant. Each team has a team leader, two riflemen, an automatic rifleman, and a grenade launcher. There are two rifle fire teams in each squad. A squad may have eight to eleven men.

Three or more squads make up a platoon. Three or more platoons make up a company. Three or more companies make up a battalion.

The XVIII Airborne Corps is the main unit containing all battalions. It is commanded by a lieutenant general (3 stars). He is assisted by a major general (2 stars) and other generals. The corps is made up of four divisions:

- 82nd Airborne Division—Carries out airborne assaults by parachuting troops into enemy areas.
- 101st Air Assault Division—Carries out airborne assaults using helicopters to drop troops into an area.
- 10th Mountain Division—Carries out any mission that takes place in a mountain region. These mountaineer soldiers can ski, climb over mountains, or rappel down mountains.
- 24th Mechanized Division—This is a motorized division. All vehicles used are on tracks. Tracked vehicles can go many places that vehicles on wheels cannot. Mechanized divisions are used to support air assaults.

Here is an example of how a division is organized. The 82nd Airborne Division is commanded by a major general, with a brigadier general to assist him. The division sergeant major has a staff of clerks to produce the paperwork required to manage the division. The division headquarters is organized into five job areas. Each area is titled "G" (for General's Staff) and given a number. These are:

G–1 – Staff paperwork, Army records, and printed orders

G–2 – Intelligence (information) gathering and study; the G-2 keeps the commander informed so that he can make military decisions

G–3 – Operations section; plans and carries out military missions

G–4 – Supply section; for equipment, vehicles, ammunition, and food

G–5 – Handles affairs with the civilian government or local people

Paratroopers in Battle

No air assault starts until the first paratrooper stands up, hooks his rip cord to the static line, and shuffles to the door. The enemy has nothing to fear until that first paratrooper touches the ground. At that point, the paratrooper is a fierce fighter and deadly weapon.

In the game of chess, the most powerful piece is the queen. The infantryman is always called the queen of battle. That's because no enemy territory is taken until an infantryman stands on the high ground. And no war is over until he meets and defeats the last resisting enemy soldier.

EARLY BATTLES

In August 1917, the 82nd Infantry Division was developed at Camp Gordon, Georgia. It included men from all over America. It was

Once paratroopers are on the ground, they become foot soldiers.

nicknamed the "All Americans." A shoulder patch was designed around the letters "AA."

The All Americans fought in France against the Germans in World War I (1914-1919). A young farmer from East Tennessee, named Alvin C. York, became its hero. York almost single-handedly killed 25 Germans, knocked out 35 machine guns, and took 132 prisoners. He won the highest medals awarded by France and Italy. He was awarded the American Medal of Honor. He also brought a lot of glory to the 82nd. Other acts of heroism added to the division's tradition. They helped to bring a quick surrender by the Germans in 1919.

After the war, the 82nd Infantry Division was broken up (deactivated). It stayed that way until 1942. In 1942, World War II was being fought. The 82nd activated again at Camp Claiborne, Louisiana. In August of 1942, the division was renamed as the 82nd Airborne Division.

Paratroopers jump in dozens at a time.

AIRBORNE MEANS "QUICK RESPONSE"

An airborne division needs to get to a battle area quickly. It is a quick-response unit. Paratroopers often are the first to go into battle. Therefore, the 82nd Airborne Division has seen action many times since 1946.

Throughout the Vietnam War (1965-1972), the 82nd saw a lot of action. They were flown into areas by helicopter and dropped onto the ground. They patrolled the jungles and assaulted enemy camps. The Vietnam War saw no huge invasions like those that happened during World War II. However, soldiers from the 82nd fought hard for their country.

In the 1970s, Middle East and African countries fought against each other many times. Although the 82nd Airborne Division did not fight, its soldiers were kept on alert (ready to go) throughout the decade.

As part of Operation Just Cause (1990) in Panama, the All Americans made their first combat jump since World War II. They jumped at night and seized control of Torrijos International Airport. This action held the airport for use by U.S. forces. The paratroopers carried out several more combat air assaults in Panama City and surrounding areas. These

Paratroopers often are the first to go into battle.

assaults were against Panamanian forces. Soldiers from the 82nd fought off the attacking forces. Panamanian President Manuel Noriega finally surrendered. The operation was a total success.

In 1990, Iraq invaded Kuwait, a neighboring country. The airborne infantry was used as a land force. They learned how to operate from armored vehicles in Saudi Arabia. They had not used vehicles before. Then they moved into Iraq. In a 100-hour-long war, the All Americans captured thousands of Iraqi troops and tons of ammunition and weapons.

From fighting in the desert, the troopers later moved into southern Florida, in 1992. Hurricane Andrew had left thousands of people homeless. A task force from Fort Bragg quickly met the people's needs for food, shelter, and medical care. These supplies were brought in both from the American Red Cross and from donations around the world.

Large military operations need hundreds of paratroopers to drop behind enemy lines.

Training 3 to Win

UNIT TRAINING CYCLES

The 82nd Airborne is the U.S. military's only paratrooper division. Therefore, it must be ready to go to any area of the world within 18 hours. The division trains while awaiting a military mission (deployment).There are three phases in the training schedule. Each brigade is in one of those phases on any given day.

MISSION CYCLE

On any day of the year, one airborne infantry brigade and one battalion of the aviation brigade are packed up and ready to move to any area of the world. Their equipment is stacked in a warehouse. It is ready to be loaded into a transport aircraft. At any moment, the paratroopers can be called away from their barracks or the mess hall to go into battle.

The 82nd Airborne is the U.S. military's only paratrooper division.

The training cycle teaches soldiers new battle tactics.

SUPPORT CYCLE

During support cycle, one brigade and one battalion of the aviation brigade help other units prepare vehicles and equipment for deployment. They support the two groups that are awaiting deployment. Once that work is complete, they assist in other areas needed at the base.

TRAINING CYCLE

The training cycle keeps the last third of the division practicing and learning new battle methods. These programs sharpen the paratrooper's combat skills.

War Games

Some training includes regular deployments to the National Training Center at Fort Irwin, California. Paratroopers train there with other military forces. They stage different kinds of mock (fake) battles. These are called war games. War games use mechanized and armored forces in realistic battle situations.

Infantry Weapons Training

Fort Bragg has seventy-five firing ranges and impact (artillery) areas. These ranges and areas are used to maintain a high level of weapons skills.

Paratroopers use the same weapons that infantrymen use. The weapons include the

bayonet, M16A2 combat rifle, .45-caliber pistol, rifle-launched and hand-thrown grenades, shoulder-fired rockets, machine guns, and mortars. New weapons are always being developed. Infantry soldiers are assured that they will use the newest, most deadly weapons available.

Hand-to-Hand Combat

Hand-to-hand combat training teaches Asian styles of fighting. This training is mixed with a back-alley style of fighting found in tough neighborhoods of big cities. Many foreign soldiers are very good at using the same techniques. However, paratroopers usually are taller, stronger, and more skilled at fighting than the enemies they meet.

The fundamentals of hand-to-hand combat are learned in basic training. However, an airborne soldier learns advanced fighting skills while in service. Hand-to-hand combat becomes his instinctive reaction to any threat.

Paratroopers are some of the toughest soldiers in the military.

LIFE AS A PARATROOPER

Infantry Fighting Strategy

The Army calls paratroopers airborne infantry soldiers. That's because once the paratrooper is on the ground, he fights like any other infantry soldier. Airborne infantrymen say they fight harder, because jump training destroys a man's tendency to be afraid of things. Any regular infantryman would be glad to know that an airborne unit was joining up with him for a ground attack.

PARATROOPERS SET AN EXAMPLE

Except during battle, you will never see sloppy paratroopers. In battle, they wear baggy uniforms that have many pockets on the legs and arms. Those are needed for carrying maps, a compass, grenades, ammunition, and rations (food).

Off the battlefield, the paratrooper tradition is to wear uniforms with razor-sharp creases. Trousers are bloused into special jump boots.

Paratroopers carry a lot of gear when going on a mission.

These boots gleam like black mirrors. Their brass glistens and their jump wings flash in the sun. Everything about their manner and dress is flawless. Paratroopers are a perfect example of military pride.

Looking into the Future

As the only airborne infantry division in the Army, the 82nd Airborne has an important mission. The ability of its soldiers to learn new fighting methods keeps it an important group. For example, in the Persian Gulf, division troops quickly learned to operate and use armored vehicles to achieve great victories. Their ability to adapt and learn so quickly made them valuable. Therefore, the 82nd will be making armored vehicle operations a part of their regular training cycles.

Some experts say it's better to put soldiers on the ground by helicopter. The 101st Air Assault Division uses helicopters. However, it takes a very long time for wave after wave of helicopters to swoop in and drop their twelve-to-fourteen-men-per-chopper load. Then they must go back to the rear and pick up another load.

After landing, a paratrooper must collect his parachute.

LIFE AS A PARATROOPER

By contrast, the 82nd recently put 204 para-troopers on the ground, with 55 tons of equipment, in fewer than 30 minutes. In the future, that time will be cut even more.

What might happen soon is the combining of airborne and air assault capability into one unit. In some ways, that has already happened. For example, the 75th Ranger Regiment is not an airborne unit. Yet all of its troops are para-troopers. It's not an air assault unit, but it often uses helicopters from the 160th Special Operations Aviation Regiment.

Both the airborne division and the air assault division probably will remain as they are for many years. That's because the United States still faces many threats in different parts of the world. The best way to combat them is with a tough, mobile, highly trained combat unit. The 82nd Airborne Division has never met its match.

No one can match the 82nd Airborne!

New Words

airborne a soldier or unit that is paratrooper qualified (see paratrooper)

barracks a military building for housing military people

chopper any type of helicopter

deactivated removed from the active group of units

deployment to put into use or action, or, positioned in an area, ready to do battle

division a large military group that includes soldiers, weapons, and vehicles

enemy territory territory occupied by enemy troops or populated by people sympathetic to the enemy side

front line a line of manned trenches and bunkers, for holding off an enemy attack

New Words

infantry foot soldiers

jump school a three-week training course that teaches recruits how to jump from airplanes and land safely using parachutes

parachute a device that uses a large cloth connected to cords and a body harness used to safely land a person jumping from an airplane

paratrooper a soldier that parachutes into battle from an airplane or helicopter

rappel to make a controlled drop, by rope, from a helicopter, cliff, or building

task force a group that is assigned a job or mission to accomplish

For Further Reading

Green, Michael. *The United States Army.* Mankato, MN: Capstone Press, Incorporated, 1998.

Hole, Dorothy. *The Army & You.* Parsippany, NJ: Silver Burdett Press, 1993.

Kurtz, Henry I. *The U.S. Army.* Brookfield, CT: Millbrook Press, Incorporated, 1993.

Rottman, Gordon. *U.S. Army Special Forces: Airborne Rangers.* Danbury, CT: Franklin Watts Incorporated, 1999.

Resources

Regional Recruiting Stations
Midwest
Chicago West Addison Recruiting Station
2550 West Addison Street
Chicago, IL 60618
(773) 327-0070

West
Los Angeles Recruiting Station
1020 South Main Street
Los Angeles, CA 90015
(213) 748-7623

East
New York Lincoln Center Recruiting Station
141 West 72nd Street
New York, NY 10023
(212) 787-0404

South
Oak Cliff Recruiting Station
620 Wynnewood Village
Dallas, TX 75224
(214) 941-1534

Resources

Web sites
Aero.com - Parachutes
www.aero.com/publications/parachutes/parachut.htm
This site contains articles, historical information, and news about parachuting. It also gives instructions on how to make your own parachute.

Army and Army Reserve Recruiting
www.goarmy.com
Official site of the U.S. Army. Take a virtual tour and learn about training, benefits, and recruiting.

U.S. Army Center of Military History
103 Third Avenue
Fort McNair, D.C. 20319-5058
www.army.mil/cmh-pg/default.htm
Dedicated to recording the history of the U.S. Army.

Index

Index

About the Author

Robert C. Kennedy entered the U.S. Army at age seventeen and attended various specialized schools. He served with a military intelligence detachment during the Korean War and with a special operations detachment during the Vietnam War, in 1967. He ended his career as an instructor for the Military Intelligence Officer Advanced Course, which he helped to develop, in 1968.